What Do You Like to Do?

Seed Learning

What do you like to do?

I like to cook.

I like to cook eggs.

What do you like to do?

I like to eat.

I like to eat sausages.

What do you like to do?

I like to play.

I like to play games.

What do you like to do?

I like to sing.

I like to sing songs.

What do you like to do?

I like to paint.

I like to paint people.

What do you like to do?

I like to drink.

I like to drink
smoothies.

What do you like to do?

I like to write.

I like to write stories.

Let's learn more about Hajj.

Color the symbol of Islam.